Robin McGraw's
Complete Makeover Guide

D0047384

Robin McGraw's
Complete Makeover Guide

Robin McGraw

THOMAS NELSON
Since 1798

NASHVILLE   DALLAS   MEXICO CITY   RIO DE JANEIRO   BEIJING

Robin McGraw's Complete Makeover Guide

© 2009 by Robin McGraw

Published in Nashville, Tennessee, by Thomas Nelson. Thomas Nelson is a registered trademark of Thomas Nelson, Inc.

Thomas Nelson, Inc., titles may be purchased in bulk for educational, business, fund-raising, or sales promotional use. For information, please e-mail SpecialMarkets@ThomasNelson.com.

Library of Congress Cataloging-in-Publication Available

ISBN 978-1-4002-0251-5

Printed in the United States of America

09 10 11 12 13 RRD 5 4 3 2 1

Contents

How to Use
This Makeover Guide

Okay, ladies, it's time to get practical.

Your age? I can only guess.

Maybe you're in your twenties: a college student, trying to make ends meet while you juggle the demands of school and work. Or maybe you're a working mother, grappling with the challenges of parenting, marriage, homemaking, and your career. Perhaps you're a single mother—all the more difficult.

Maybe you're a thirty-something working hard for your next promotion or career change. Your days are long, your boss expects a lot from you, and somehow you're doing it all . . . including keeping your townhome clean.

Perhaps you're in your forties, with a houseful of teenagers. You're a soccer mom, a wrestling mom, a cheerleading mom, and the cochair of your local PTA. You're trying to keep a clean house, put balanced meals on the table, make it to every school event—and keep your job! You're doing your level best to keep everyone happy, healthy, and thriving.

Maybe you're in your fifties, sixties, or beyond with an empty nest but a hectic career. All that and you're battling the symptoms of menopause too.

Whatever your age, you and I have something in common: we're women, we're busy, and we want to look and feel our best, no matter what our age.

That's what this book is about.

Robin McGraw's Complete Makeover Guide is designed to be a companion to *What's Age Got to Do with It?* If you have not yet read this book, I encourage you to pick it up immediately to read alongside this workbook. In *What's Age Got to Do with It?* you will find tons of helpful information that you can use to help you look and feel your very best at any age.

Each chapter in this workbook contains a specific reading assignment from *What's Age Got to Do with It?* Additionally, in answer to questions from readers like you, I have provided health and beauty tips in an easy-to-follow format. Finally, I have included a number of quizzes, self-tests, checklists, and other application tools you can customize to meet your specific, everyday needs to help you achieve your optimal health and beauty.

Features of
Robin McGraw's Complete Makeover Guide

Q&A: Questions that readers like you have asked about beauty, health, fitness, fashion, and aging, with answers based on solid research and personal experience.

Reading Assignments: A reading assignment from the book *What's Age Got to Do with It?*

Resources: Reproducible forms, charts, and lists that you can personalize, such as a basic fitness log, shopping lists, a meal planning register, a wardrobe-building shopping tool, skin type quiz, and more.

In short, this guide is designed to be a handy, personalized, all-in-one tool you can use to help you make all of your glamour and wellness decisions and document them along the way.

Now let's get started!

What's Age Got to Do with It?

Before we begin to discuss the topics of fitness, skin care, fashion, and so on, I'd like to answer what is probably the most common question I hear from women everywhere:

Q: How can I stop the effects of aging?

A: Here's the bare fact: you will age. From the moment we are born, we are already aging, and aging can never be stopped. But the good news is, the effects of aging can be minimized and, in some cases, reversed. The physical signs of aging can be reduced by making wise lifestyle choices with your nutrition, sleep, beauty, and more.

Let's look at some of the things that add the appearance of age and zap years from our lives:

Things That Age Our Skin

- sun exposure
- sugar (see chapter 3 in *What's Age Got to Do with It?*)
- processed foods
- harsh chemicals
- improper cleansing
- saturated and trans fats
- insufficient sleep
- stress
- smoking
- dehydration
- acne

Things That Age Our Bodies

- weak immune system
- disease
- stress
- smoking
- alcohol
- drug use
- inadequate diet/ vitamin and mineral deficiencies
- excess weight
- insufficient sleep

Things That Age Our Overall Appearance

- "old" clothing (that is, clothing meant for someone older than you)
- outdated clothing
- poor posture
- the same things that age our skin and bodies

The information and tools in this makeover guide will help you fight the appearance of old age while highlighting your authentic, beautiful self.

READING ASSIGNMENT

Chapter 1 from *What's Age Got to Do with It?*

Before we close this introductory chapter, I'd like for you to do an aging inventory. Below you will find a "How Am I Aging?" assessment. Please be honest as you take this test . . .

How Am I Aging?

Place a check in the box for each statement that is true for you.

	I spend a lot of time in the sun, without sunscreen.
	I eat a lot of sweets and/or processed foods (canned/boxed prepared meals, lunch meats, etc., particularly those with MSG and/or sodium nitrate/nitrates).
	I wash my face with bar soap.
	I use rubbing alcohol on my skin, as an astringent.

	I go to bed with my makeup on.
	I have acne.
	My diet is high in saturated and trans fats.
	I eat a lot of deep-fried foods.
	My job is very high-stress.
	I am suffering a lot of personal stress.
	I am very unhappy and unfulfilled.
	I cry a lot.
	I am a smoker.
	I stay up late and get up early.
	I am sick a lot (colds, flu, etc.).
	I have a diagnosed disease.
	I drink alcohol.
	I drink more than one alcoholic beverage a day
	I am a drug user.
	I am overweight.

I take a multivitamin every day.	
I eat a balanced diet.	

I am very physically fit, and I exercise at least 30 minutes a day, three times a week or more.	
I stand tall and erect.	
My wardrobe is fashionable and up-to-date.	
I am a happy person, and I laugh a lot.	
I use a good skin care system, day and night.	
I avoid foods with monosodium glutamate and/or sodium nitrite/nitrate.	
I get 8 hours of sleep (or more) a night.	
I drink eight 8-ounce glasses (or more) of water daily.	
I usually or always wear sunscreen during the daylight hours.	
I eat a lot of green, leafy vegetables.	
I eat a lot of whole foods.	
I have at least one bowel movement a day and never have to use laxatives.	
I avoid sweets and excess caffeine.	
I enjoy warm, healthy relationships at home and with friends and coworkers.	
I feel fulfilled in my work and my life (place two checks if you love your job).	
I don't let things "get to me."	
I don't smoke or drink.	
Drugs? Not me!	

Now, examine the results from the "How Am I Aging?" assessment. If your right-hand column is full of checks, congratulations! You will most likely age with grace. You probably already look younger than your same-age friends and acquaintances. But if the majority of checks are in the left-hand column . . . you may want to think carefully about how you really want to look in five, ten, fifteen years. You have already done some damage and are continuing to add years to your appearance—and you may be cutting years from your life.

But that's what we're here for, right? In the next chapter, we are going to start by looking at fitness and discover how exercise can play a part in helping you look and feel your best at any age.

2

What's Fitness Got to Do with It?

As you have already discovered, how old you look today and how well you will age in the years to come is directly related to your level of fitness. One thing that is key to every woman's fitness is exercise, so I'd like to begin this chapter by answering a very important question:

Q: How can exercise help combat the aging process?

A: Studies suggest that regular exercise can reduce your risk of diseases such as heart disease, cancer, diabetes, and osteoporosis; improve cholesterol, blood pressure, insomnia, and depression; and strengthen your immune system, among many other benefits. . . . Because exercise increases circulation throughout the body, it can give your skin a youthful glow.

—from *What's Age Got to Do with It?*[1]

READING ASSIGNMENT

Chapter 2 from *What's Age Got to Do with It?*

Now, you may be saying, "Okay, you've convinced me. I need to exercise. But I don't even know where to begin." Let me start with a quick review of some tips I shared in *What's Age Got to Do with It?*

Schedule your workouts

Write down or put into your BlackBerry the days and times you plan to work out. This makes it a nonnegotiable event. You'll be less likely to skip it.

Buddy up

Often, working out with another person often improves the chances that you'll stick with it.

Consult with the experts

Invest in at least a couple of sessions with an expert who can show you proper form and exercises that will help you reach your goals. Or you can talk with friends or family members who are avid exercisers.

Take notes

Write down when you're going to exercise and what you plan to do when you exercise. Then record each workout in the Basic Fitness Log provided in this guide. What did you do? How many reps did you do? How long did you exercise? What did you do? How did you feel?

Tell others about your new fitness regimen

Telling others helps you stay accountable. Those who are aware of your get-fit plan will keep you honest.

Set a goal

Whether your goal is losing five pounds, running a 5K race, or just improving your fitness level, having a goal gives you something to strive for. It is also important to have a target date. For example:

"I want to lose 30 pounds by Christmas."
"I want to be a size _____ by my class reunion the weekend of _____."

In addition to long-term goals, set smaller ones too. For example:

"This week, I want to strength train three times."
"Today, I want to run two minutes longer than yesterday."

Let's get practical now. You've made the decision to begin a fitness regimen. Now you will make some choices, based on the list I just gave you, to help you exercise for success. Please fill in the blanks on the "My Fitness Plan" form that follows:

My Fitness Plan

Days I Will Exercise	Time	Type of Exercise
Sunday	_____	_____
Monday	_____	_____
Tuesday	_____	_____
Wednesday	_____	_____
Thursday	_____	_____
Friday	_____	_____
Saturday	_____	_____

I will exercise with:

[Name] _____ on [day(s) of week] _____

[Name] _____ on [day(s) of week] _____

I will consult with:

_____

_____

_____

Long-term goals

I will _____

by _____ (date)

I will _____

by _____ (date)

I will _____

by _____ (date)

Short-term goals

By (date) _____ I will _____.

By (date) _____ I will _____.

By (date) _____ I will _____.

By (date) _____ I will _____.

By (date) _____ I will _____.

Who I'll Tell

I will tell these people about my fitness plan and goals

_____ _____

_____ _____

I will be accountable to

_____ _____

_____ _____

Some exercises I would like to try

_____

_____

Today's Date _____

Measurements

Current weight _____   Bust _____

Goal weight _____   Hips _____

My pants size _____   Waist _____

Goal pants size _____   Biceps _____

My bra size _____

Goal bra size _____

My shirt size _____

Goal shirt size _____

Before You Begin . . .

It should go without saying that before you begin any exercise program, you should consult your physician. In addition to this, another "first" has to do with something that is of the utmost importance: posture.

In chapter 2 of *What's Age Got to Do with It?*, I told the story of the day I noticed my husband's hunched-over posture as he was walking across the stage. It made him look older than his years.[2] Indeed, bad posture does make you look older and heavier, while good posture can make you look at least five pounds slimmer. But good posture is also important in your exercise routine, and no routine can give you the look you want when it is performed day after day with substandard posture. Even the slimmest and best-toned body looks years older when that body is slumped.

Here's a quick review of the simple Pilates move that can help you stand taller, both on the exercise mat and in day-to-day life:

1. Clasp your hands behind your back.
2. Pull your clasped hands down toward the floor so that your shoulders go back and down.

Doesn't that feel better? It certainly looks better. This is the posture you should maintain as you sit, stand, walk, or perform any seated or standing exercise. By the way, this is what Phillip did, and now he looks ten years younger!

Q: How can I measure my success?

A: Having already read chapter 2 in *What's Age Got to Do with It?*, you know that I work with a personal trainer named

Robert Reames. In that chapter, Robert recommended several ways to measure your exercise progress. Though I tend to measure progress by how my clothes fit, you may also find the following tips from Robert helpful:

- On the bathroom scale
- By taking measurements of your body with a tape measure
- Using an item of clothing regularly to check for body changes
- A basic fitness test, taken at the beginning of your exercise program, to establish your baseline fitness level. (See chapter 2, under "Answers from the Expert," for a list of the activities you will complete during this exercise.[3]) This basic fitness test should be repeated monthly.

On the next page I have provided a form for you to chart the results of your first Basic Fitness Test. Feel free to photocopy this form as often as you like to use each month when you chart your progress.

Each time you complete the Basic Fitness Test, you will also post your results on the Basic Fitness Log that immediately follows the Basic Fitness Test.

Finally, you'll also find there a Fitness Program Progress Log. This log is different from the Basic Fitness Log in that it is only used to record your weight and measurements. You will not record the activity results from the Basic Fitness Test on the Fitness Program Progress Log.

Basic Fitness Test

This test is designed to help you determine your baseline fitness level. Please follow the directions below, and record your times and numbers in the spaces provided. Repeat this monthly.

Note: As you complete this initial fitness test, make sure that you are exerting yourself in the same way you would during any normal exercise session. The key is not in overdoing it for the sake of a great initial work-out. It is in honestly assessing your current fitness level so you can accurately monitor your long-term progress.

Today's Date: _____

1. For one minute, see how many chair squats you can do. Stand in front of a chair with feet shoulder-width apart and arms by your sides. With most of your weight on your heels, squat down as if you're about to sit in the chair, but return to standing just as your rear grazes the chair.

   I did _____ chair squats in 60 seconds.

2. For one minute, see how many push-ups you can do. If you can't do a standard push-up, then do wall push-ups where you stand about an arm's length from the wall with hands shoulder-width apart at shoulder height.

   I did _____ push-ups in 60 seconds.

3. Walk or run one mile as fast as you can.

Today I (walked) (ran) one mile in _____ (time).

4. Test your balance by standing on one leg and timing yourself. Switch legs and repeat.

I balanced myself on my left leg for _____ (time).

I balanced myself on my right leg for _____ (time).

Measurements

Current weight _____   Bust _____

Goal weight   _____   Hips _____

My pants size _____   Waist _____

Goal pants size _____   Biceps _____

My bra size _____

Goal bra size _____

My shirt size _____

Goal shirt size _____

Basic Fitness Log

Date	Chair Squats (number)	Push-ups	One-Mile Walk/Run (record time)	Time balanced on left leg	Time balanced on right leg
Starting date:					
(1 month from starting date)					
(2 months)					
(3 months)					
(4 months)					
(5 months)					
(6 months)					
(7 months)					
(8 months)					
(9 months)					
(10 months)					
(11 months)					
(1 year from start date)					

Fitness Program Progress Log

Weight	Pant size	Bra size	Shirt size	Bust	Waist	Hips	Biceps

*This form is reproducible

A Word of Caution

As I shared with you in chapter 2 of *What's Age Got to Do with It?*, Robert confirms that one of the biggest mistakes women make when exercising is concentrating solely or excessively on cardio exercises. Cardio burns fat, true, and it's good for your heart. But strength training is important too. You need to provide some form of resistance for your muscles. Review chapter 2 for ways to add strength training to your exercise program. Remember that when you combine cardio and strength training, you will be successful at both chronic calorie burning (burning calories while your body is at rest) and acute calorie burning (calories burned during exercise and for a couple of hours after).

ACTIVITY	CALORIES BURNED PER HALF HOUR*
Bicycling (leisure)	108
Dishwashing	61
Grocery shopping	65
High-impact aerobics	191
Horseback riding (leisurely)	68
Ironing	61
Low-impact aerobics	166
Pilates (beginner level)	101
Running (slow pace)	490
Sex (10 minutes)	38
Vacuuming	79
Walking the dog	107

* Based on a weight of 120 pounds

Start on the Right Foot!

Now it's time to make a plan and put that plan into action. Below I have provided a sample reproducible Daily Exercise Journal that you can use to document your workouts.

As you fill out the journal, be specific. What kinds of exercises did you perform? How many reps did you do? How did you feel when your workout was done? Don't forget to thank your body for the hard work that it did!

Daily Exercise Journal

Cardio	
Strength Training	
Total Time Spent	
How I Felt After Workout	
Things to Celebrate	

WORKOUT EQUIPMENT AND GEAR

While successful exercise does not require special or expensive gear, there are some items that may be helpful to have. Put a check mark beside any of the items below that you would like to purchase:

☐ Bathroom scale
☐ Stopwatch/timer
☐ Heart rate monitor
☐ Measuring tape
☐ Dumbbells (5-, 8-, 10-, and 12-pound)
☐ Hand/wrist weights
☐ Ankle weights
☐ Exercise videos/DVDs
☐ Music CDs for aerobic exercise
☐ Good pair of walking/running shoes
☐ Floor mat
☐ Stretching bands
☐ Exercise ball

You're Getting Sleepy . . . Sleeeeepy

Now that we've discussed the role of exercise in fitness, there's another critical fitness element: sleep. Most experts say that women need between seven and nine hours of restful sleep. Sleep shortened and interrupted by constant wakeups, whether due to anxiety, external factors (such as a howling cat or a crying baby), trips to the bathroom, or night sweats, will not do your body or mind the good that extended, uninterrupted, and body-relaxing sleep will. How's your sleep?

Are you having difficulty sleeping? Do you have a hard time winding down at night and getting to sleep? Do you wake up frequently? Too early? What's keeping you up at night? And how do you feel in the morning? Rested? Or just as exhausted as you were when your head hit the pillow the night before? Do you hit that snooze button five times in a row because you just can't get out of bed? Or do you spring from your mattress, ready to take on the world?

If you believe that your sleep patterns may be adversely affecting your health and life performance, it may be time to take some notes and possibly even speak to your physician about it. On the following pages, you will find a Weekly Sleep Journal you can use to document your sleep patterns. If you're already sleeping well and you wake up feeling refreshed each day, great! But if you're having trouble, this log may provide you and your doctor the answers you need to help you get the rest that your body requires to function at its peak.

Weekly Sleep Journal

Week of _____

(date)

Day	Hours Slept (total nightly)	Specific Time Range (ex.: from _:00 to _:00)		How long it took me to fall asleep
		Bedtime	Wake time	
SUNDAY				
MONDAY				
TUESDAY				
WEDNESDAY				
THURSDAY				
FRIDAY				
SATURDAY				

How many times I woke up/got up during the night	Nap(s) taken during the day (ex.: from _:00 to _:00)	Food(s) eaten within 5 hours of bedtime

*This form is reproducible

(PART TWO OF SLEEP JOURNAL)

Day	Alcohol or caffeinated beverages consumed before bedtime	Medications (names and dosages)	How I felt at bedtime (calm, depressed, anxious, stressed, etc.)
Sunday			
Monday			
Tuesday			
Wednesday			
Thursday			
Friday			
Saturday			

Things that may have been on my mind	How I felt on waking in the morning, on a scale of 1 to 10 (with 1 being utterly exhausted and 10 being refreshed and ready to take on the world)	I woke up _____ (naturally, to an alarm, etc.)

Troubling sleep patterns that I notice: _____

_____

_____

_____

Things I may want to discuss with my doctor: _____

_____

_____

_____

Ready, Set . . . Eat?

Yes, eat. Sleep is a wonderful thing, and we need to get enough of it if we're going to look and feel on top of the world. Yet we'll feel sluggish when we wake up if we don't properly feed our "machines." Exercise is beneficial, too, and I'm glad you've committed to a conscientious workout program. But no amount of exercise can make up for a body that is poorly fed and deficient in critical vitamins and minerals.

In the next chapter, we will talk about how to feed that sleek, toned, well-rested female physique of yours. So pick up your fork, ladies. It's time to chow down!

3

What's Nutrition Got to Do with It?

Every morning, Christy would rise at the crack of dawn, get herself presentable, don her workout clothing, stuff her work clothes into a duffel bag, and head for the gym.

"Aren't you going to have breakfast?" her concerned husband would call out.

"No, honey. Don't have time," she'd respond, her voice already distant to her husband's ears.

At the gym, she would work out feverishly. An hour and a half later, muscles pumped and face flushed, she'd head for the shower, already running a bit late for work.

Once there, the pace is hectic. Meetings. Agendas. Fires to put out. Before she knows it, it's lunchtime. *No time to eat*, she muses, grabbing a Snickers bar from the vending machine.

Five o'clock comes, and she can't leave. Her fires are still smoldering, and if she doesn't douse them, who will? Six o'clock arrives, and there are still embers, but by six thirty, the coast is clear. She gets in her car and begins the thirty-minute drive home.

On her way home, she knows she's too tired to cook. She swings by the drive-through and grabs a sack of burgers, fries, and two soft drinks for her and her husband. Minutes later, she breezes through her front door, wolfs down dinner, and crashes for the night after a long day.

The next morning comes, and it's "second verse, same as the first."

Christy wonders why her hair has no luster, her skin breaks out, and her nails are brittle. She's perpetually exhausted—it's easy to blame work—and she catches every cold and virus that comes her way. What Christy doesn't know is that she's suffering from a nutrition malfunction, and her health and appearance will only get worse.

READING ASSIGNMENT

Chapter 3 from *What's Age Got to Do with It?*

Nutrition

I can't say enough about the importance of what you put into your body. You can get all of the other things right—good sleep, adequate exercise— but if you are not feeding your body the things it needs to function, your face will show it and your health will deteriorate. That's why I'd like to begin this chapter by answering an all-important question about nutrition.

Q: What kinds of foods should I eat in order to be healthy?

A: The U.S. Department of Agriculture (USDA) has developed a "Food Guide Pyramid" to help consumers make wise decisions regarding the types of foods they need to eat.[1] Though individuals are meant to customize the pyramid according to their gender, age, height and weight, activity level, etc., the basic plan recommends:

> 6–11 servings of breads and grains
> 2–4 servings of fruits
> 3–5 servings of vegetables
> 2–3 servings of dairy
> 2–3 servings of protein

The breads and grains group includes things such as cereals, pasta, rice (preferably brown or wild), bagels, couscous, etc. Whenever possible, choose whole-wheat or whole-grain versions of these foods.

Eat fruits and vegetables raw as often as possible, and make as many "high-color" selections as you can: bright-red strawberries, bright-yellow peppers, blueberries, and so on. Also, try to eat green, leafy vegetables. Make sure to include cruciferous vegetables (broccoli, cabbage, cauliflower, etc.).

Proteins include dry beans, nuts and seeds, meats and fish, and eggs. Always choose lean cuts of meat, and avoid frying. Nuts are very calorie dense, so be careful how much you eat of them.

The dairy group includes milk, cheese, and yogurt. Go nonfat or low fat whenever possible when eating dairy. Avoid ice cream as much as you can, opting instead for ice milk or low-fat frozen yogurt.

How can you make sure you're getting enough of all the right things? Below is a worksheet that you can use to track foods you eat from each group. At the end of the day, you'll know whether you've satisfied the USDA's requirements for a healthy body.

In the appropriate column below, list each of the items you have eaten today from each food group.

Daily Food Groups Consumption Sheet

Bread/ Grains (6–11 servings)	Fruits (2–4 servings)	Vegetables (3–5 servings)	Proteins (2–3 servings)	Dairy (2–3 servings)

In the bread group, I was short _____ servings.

In the fruits group, I was short _____ servings.

In the vegetables group, I was short _____ servings.

In the dairy group, I was short _____ servings.

In the protein group, I was short _____ servings.

How'd you do? If you didn't fare so well the first day you logged your food-groups consumption, don't despair. Try again, and be creative as you seek to fill your diet with the right amounts of the right foods.

STUFF TO AVOID

Sugar/sweets	MSG (monosodium glutamate)
Soda	Sodium nitrite and other nitrates
Imitation sweeteners	Oils, trans fats, saturated fats
Processed foods	

Q: What if I need to lose weight? Do I still need to eat all of those servings?

A: Whether you need to lose weight, maintain your current weight, or gain weight, you still need to consume the right amounts of all of the food groups on the pyramid. But if losing weight specifically is one of your goals, you're going to have to cut calories at the same time.

Q: How can I know how many calories are in the foods I eat?

A: Personally, I don't put a lot of emphasis on calorie counting. But if you are interested in finding out, there are many excellent tools out there to help women count calories. Supermarket checkout stands abound with various "pocket calorie counters." In addition, bookstores carry larger calorie guides, brand-name calorie counters, and other options. Two very good books to have are Corinne T. Netzer's *The Complete Book of Food Counts* and *The Calorie King Calorie, Fat, and Carbohydrate Counter* (both of these also have carbohydrate, protein, cholesterol, fat gram, and sodium counts).[2] The first of these is perfect for your kitchen, and the second is just the right size to carry in your purse.

But there are also very helpful websites, such as calorie countercharts.com, which sorts foods alphabetically and lists calories, and www.caloriescount.org, which offers the Calorie Control Council's "Enhanced Calorie Calculator," in which the dieter simply enters a food name in the keyword box and clicks on the Submit Food Item(s) button to get the number of calories in that food.

Q: I eat out a lot. How can I find the calories in restaurant food?

A: Many books and websites feature special sections containing the calorie counts for many popular restaurants, including fast-food chains. And if that's not enough, most major restaurant chains have online nutrition information. One website, dietfacts.com, has an extensive list of restaurants that you can choose from. When you click on the restaurant's name, you are given a list of menu offerings. You can get the nutrition facts for any item on the list.

BEST ANTIOXIDANTS

blueberries	cherries	black beans
pomegranates	raspberries	acai berries
cranberries	apples	goji berries

Q: What's your best advice for dieting?

A: As I've said before, "dieting" doesn't work. Instead, you have to commit to a lifestyle that supports day-to-day healthy eating. But if you also want to lose weight, you have to eat the right foods in the right amounts, making sure that you are not consuming more calories than you can burn.

So, how do you know how many calories you need per day? Determining a specific individual's calorie needs can be complex. Factors include age, gender, metabolism, activity level, and so on. But there is a simple formula that can be adjusted up or down for just about any active woman.

Current Weight   _____   (write in your current weight)

              x 12   (multiply your weight times twelve)

_____   (maintenance calories)

This is the number of calories you need to maintain your current weight. To determine how many calories you should eat if you want to lose weight,

Maintenance calories   _____   (enter the total from above)

            – 500   (subtract 500 from this number)

_____   (goal calorie count for weight loss)

Based on this formula, on the next page I have provided a chart showing different weights and the number of calories necessary to maintain each.

Weight (lbs.)	Calories Needed to Maintain Weight	Calories Needed to Lose Weight	Calories Needed to Gain Weight
120	1440	940	1940
125	1500	1000	2000
130	1560	1060	2060
135	1620	1120	2120
140	1680	1180	2180
145	1740	1240	2240
150	1800	1300	2300
155	1860	1360	2360
160	1920	1420	2420
165	1980	1480	2480
170	2040	1540	2540
175	2100	1600	2600
180	2160	1660	2660
185	2220	1720	2720
190	2280	1780	2780
195	2340	1840	2840
200	2400	1900	2900

Thankfully, for people who simply have no idea how to begin a weight-loss program, my husband has created a fourteen-day Rapid Start Plan. If you need to cut pounds but don't know how to plan a low-fat, lower-calorie menu, I highly recommend that you follow the Rapid Start Plan that I have included at the end of chapter 3 in *What's Age Got to Do with It?* (pages 65–77; the Rapid Start Plan was originally published in Phillip's *The Ultimate Weight Solution Food Guide*). The meals listed in that kick-start program are appropriately portioned and nutritionally balanced (which that means you'll be pleased at the end of the day if you have used your Daily Food Groups Consumption Sheet, provided on page 30). By following this healthy food plan for two weeks, you'll get a sense of proper portion size. That, ladies, is information you can use for life.

For more help with weight loss, I recommend that you read Phillip's *The Ultimate Weight Solution Food Guide*.[3] In it you'll find everything you need to know to learn how to eat for life.

Here are some tips for successful weight loss that I share in *What's Age Got to Do with It?*:

- Try not to skip meals. (Especially breakfast!)
- Plan your meals. (Every single one.)
- Keep a food diary. (Don't cheat; your journal won't know, but your hips will.)
- Choose smaller dishes. (The six-inch plate instead of the ten-inch.)
- Make healthy substitutions. (Skim milk, not whole.)

- Read food labels. (Half of that Otis Spunkmeyer muffin, ladies, not the whole thing!)

- Drink enough water. (A minimum of eight 8-ounce glasses a day—more if you work out hard.)

- Flush yourself out. (Eat natural-diuretic fruits and vegetables.)

- Sip green tea. (A natural fat burner.)

- Skip the soda. (It's bad for your bones anyway.)

Now that you've read chapter 3 in *What's Age Got to Do with It?* along with this chapter, you've got a fairly good idea that planning your meals ahead of time is important. On the next page, you'll find a sample Meal Planning Register, with a preplanned menu filled in. This sample will show you how to use the register for yourself. There is also a Weekly Meal Planning Register for those of you who would like to plan your meals in advance for a week (recommended).

Meal Planning Register (sample)

Today I will eat:

Time of Day	Foods	Calories per item	Calories
Breakfast	Black coffee	0	230
	½ papaya, cubed	70	
	poached egg	70	
	1 slice whole-wheat toast with 1 tsp butter	90	
Midmorning snack	Sliced apple (med)	80	280
	1 oz. walnuts	200	
Lunch	Turkey sandwich made with 2 oz. white-meat turkey, 2 slices whole-wheat bread, sliced tomato, lettuce, alfalfa sprouts, mustard	260	430
	1 cup grapes	80	
	1 cup skim milk	90	
	green tea	0	
Afternoon snack	Slice of whole-wheat toast with 1 T. honey	135	135
Supper	1 boneless, skinless chicken breast half (approx. 4 oz.), baked or broiled	140	375
	1 baked potato (about 2 inches in diameter) with 2 T. nonfat sour cream	165	
	salad made with lettuce, sliced green and red pepper, sliced cucumber, and 2 T. vinaigrette	70	
	cold green tea	0	
Dinner	1 small container (5.3 oz) Greek yogurt		110

Total calories for the day 1560*

*Note: Any moderately active woman weighing more than 130 pounds will lose weight eating this number of calories

Meal Planning Register

Today I will eat:

Time of Day	Foods	Calories per item	Calories
Breakfast			
Midmorning snack			
Lunch			
Afternoon snack			
Supper			
Dinner			

Total calories for the day 1560*

Total calories for the day _____

*Note: Any moderately active woman weighing more than 130 pounds will lose weight
eating this number of calories per day.

**This form is reproducible.

Weekly Meal Planning Register

Bread/ Grains (6–11 servings)	Fruits (2–4 servings)	Vegetables (3–5 servings)	Proteins (2–3 servings)	Dairy (2–3 servings)

*This form is reproducible.

SUGGESTED SHOPPING LIST FOR EFFECTIVE DIETING

☐ bathroom scale

☐ tape measure

☐ food scale (preferably electronic)

☐ calorie book (may also include counts for fat grams, carbs, etc.)

☐ measuring spoon set (don't cheat with these!)

☐ measuring cup set

SUPPLEMENTS: A RECIPE FOR SUCCESS

Take: 1 multivitamin

Add: A supplement containing 400 milligrams calcium and 400 IU of vitamin D*

Mix with: a high-fiber, low-fat diet heavy in fruits, veggies, and whole grains, plus three glasses of milk or three servings of low-fat yogurt each day . . . for the rest of your life!

Yield: One bone-healthy female

* According to the National Osteoperosis Foundation, the recommendation is 1,000 milligrams of calcium and 400–800 IU of vitamin D for women ages 19–49 (which can be obtained easily with the combination of food, dairy, and the supplements listed above) and 1,200 mg of calcium and 800–1,000 IU of vitamin D for women over age 50.

4

What's Skin Care Got to Do with It?

L ook at you! There you are, the picture of health, the glow of good fitness emanating from your face, your cheeks rosy from all that exercise you've been doing so persistently. Speaking of cheeks, this chapter is about skin care and how you can look as young, healthy, and vibrant as you're beginning to feel.

READING ASSIGNMENT

Chapter 4 from *What's Age Got to Do with It?*

In chapter 4 of *What's Age Got to Do with It?*, I provided helpful professional and personal information about good skin care. I shared a number of my own skin care practices and preferences, as well as a variety of facial exercises, recipes for homemade treatments, and expert advice from a celebrated Beverly Hills aesthetician. The chapter also contained good questions and answers in relation to skin care. Here I want you to get down to basics and determine what's best for you.

Q: OK, Robin, you told me about a lot of good products, and I'd like to try them all. But tell me . . . what do I really need in a skin care system? What are the bare essentials?

A: Most skin care systems, at the very least, would recommend the use of: (1) a cleanser; (2) a "toner" (these go by various names, depending on the maker: e.g., clarifier, astringent); and (3) a moisturizer. But, as I mentioned in *What's Age Got to Do with It?*, since the skin around the eyes is thinner and breaks down (read "wrinkles") more quickly than your other facial skin, I highly recommend the day-and-night use of an eye cream too. At the bare minimum, a skin care regimen should include a cleanser, a moisturizer, and an eye cream daily/nightly. Sunscreen is another must-have.

Q: Can I mix and match products from different skin care companies, or should I stick with one brand?

A: I don't recommend mixing brands. Most skin care products are designed to work best in combination with other products in that line. Mixing and matching among product lines can result in one product's key ingredient counteracting the active ingredient in another product. You may even experience side effects, such as overdrying, breakouts, or allergic reactions. My advice is to choose a skin care line and stick with it, using products from just that line. In saying that, remember to look for products that contain ingredients that stimulate the growth of collagen and protect your skin from sun damage.

SKIN DO'S

- Use sunscreen when you're out in the sun.

- Use a skin care system, day and night.

- Make sure your skin care products contain sun protection (SPF 15 or greater).

- Get your beauty sleep (most women need at least eight hours per night).

- Avoid alcohol.

- Drink plenty of water, and eat water-rich foods.

- Eat lots of fruits and veggies (particularly green, leafy vegetables).

- Once a month, examine your skin from head to toe to make sure no moles have changed in size or appearance (possible sign of skin cancer).

- Once a year, if possible, have a professional skin exam. (The American Academy of Dermatology offers free skin cancer screenings nationwide. Visit their website at aad.org for more information.)

SKIN DON'TS

Don't smoke.

Don't spend too much time in the sun.

Don't go to bed with your makeup on.

Don't use bar soap (e.g., Zest, Safeguard, Dial) to wash your face.

Don't mix products from different skin care lines.

Q: I don't know my skin type. How can I find out?

A: There are several different ways to discover your skin type. One way is to go by a department store cosmetic counter. A few minutes with a beauty adviser from any of the reputable cosmetic companies (e.g., Lancôme, Estée Lauder, Elizabeth Arden) and you will know your skin type. The beauty experts at any of these counters will ask you a series of questions about your skin. Then, coupled with their own observations, they will use your answers to determine whether you have oily, dry, normal, sensitive—or whatever—skin. Then, based on your skin type and its unique needs (say, if you have an uneven skin tone, acne, dark circles, eye puffiness, crow's feet, etc.), they can recommend a skin care regimen designed especially for you.

Another way to find out your skin type is to go online. Many companies, including some of those I mentioned in chapter 4 of *What's Age Got to Do with It?*, offer online profiling so you can find out your skin type and obtain a skin care program tailored to that type. (Some don't offer assistance finding out your skin type, but if you already know it, they can match you up with the products that are right for your needs.) Neutrogena's website, for example, offers a personal e-Valuation that asks viewers a series of questions and, in the end, suggests products that are right for them. Avon's site also offers help with product selection. The Olay website is another that provides tailored skin care routines based on your answers to their interactive Olay for You analysis.

Or third, you can take the "What's My Skin Type?" quiz offered on the next page. While I won't be offering you a specific skin care system, you will at least be able to get a fair idea of your skin type and some of the specific needs that you may want to address when choosing skin care products.

What's My Skin Type?

1. Two hours after cleansing my face in the morning . . .
   (circle one)
   a. my face is oily all over, even my cheeks.
   b. only my T-zone is oily.
   c. my face is very dry, with not a trace of oil.

2. Two hours after cleansing my face in the morning . . .
   (circle one)
   a. my whole face shines like a new penny.
   b. my forehead, the tip of my nose, and sometimes my chin are shiny.
   c. my skin doesn't shine anywhere.

3. Two hours after cleansing my face in the morning . . .
   (circle one)
   a. my skin feels greasy, but not uncomfortable.
   b. my skin just feels normal.
   c. my skin feels tight.
   d. my skin feels tight then and all day long.
   e. my skin feels coarse when I touch it.

4. My pores are . . .
   a. very large.
   b. small.
   c. invisible.

If most of your answers were a's in these first four questions, your skin is most likely oily, and you should select oily-skin products when making your skin care purchases.

If most of your answers were b's, your skin is probably normal.

If most of your answers were c's (d or e on number 3), your skin is probably dry. You will want to make sure that the cleansers you buy don't further dry out your skin and that the moisturizers you buy are powerful rehydrators.

5. My skin . . . (circle all that apply)
   a. is always broken out.
   b. breaks out when I'm under stress.
   c. breaks out only during my period.
   e. breaks out when I'm under stress, when I'm having my period, and occasionally at other times.
   f. breaks out when I use certain products.
   d. never breaks out.

6. In the sun . . .
   a. I tend to burn.
   b. I burn, but then my burn turns into a suntan.
   c. I tend to tan.
   d. I try to stay out of the sun!

7. My skin . . . (circle all that apply)
   a. is very sensitive and burns when I use most products.
   b. is very thin and transparent.
   c. clearly shows broken capillaries (often seen around the nose)

   d. is sensitive to these products (list on the lines below):

_____

_____

_____

   e. isn't sensitive at all.

If your answer to question 5 reflects that you have trouble with breakouts, you will also want to add products that treat acne. You will certainly want to be careful to avoid products that could compound the problem.

Where sun is concerned (question 6), the quicker you burn, the higher the SPF you need in your skin care products. As I said in *What's Age Got to Do with It?*, sunscreen is very important. We should choose skin care products that protect our skin from the sun's rays; those who are fairer and burn more easily need high-SPF products. (As a general rule, you get about fifteen minutes' protection for each level of SPF: SPF 4 gives an hour's protection. SPF 8, two hours' protection, and so on.)

Very thin/transparent skin or skin that shows numerous broken capillaries is often sensitive. And when the majority of products you apply cause burning, again, your skin is sensitive. You may even be allergic to one of the ingredients common to many product lines. You may then have to seek hypoallergenic skin care treatments or even physician's products.

And finally, skin that has dry patches, flakiness, or an overall dull appearance may require an exfoliating product to slough off dead skin cells.

Put Your Best Face Forward

You and I should use our skin care products faithfully, day and night, and we need to give them time to work. If you need line correction, blotch correction, or age spot correction, you can't start on a skin care regime on Monday and expect to look ten years younger by Friday. And as the purpose of this chapter is to encourage you to begin or continue a lifelong skin care program—not to promote products—I encourage you to do your homework. Go online. Visit the cosmetic counters. Read the labels. Then make informed choices based on your unique skin.

The choices are endless, so where should you start?

Here's a little something that will help you out. On the next page, write in all of the skin care products you'd like to try. What would you like to find out more about? Which product ads appeal to you? Write all of that down on the following "Skin Care Options I'd Like to Try" worksheet, and use it as a sort of shopping list when it's time to start making purchases.

Skin Care Options I'd Like to Try

Company ads/commercials that pique my interest:

_____

_____

_____

_____

Cosmetic counters I'd like to visit:

_____

_____

_____

_____

Salon treatments/facials I'd like to learn more about:

_____

_____

_____

_____

Skin care company websites I'd like to explore:

_____

_____

_____

_____

Cleansers I'd like to try:

_____

_____

_____

_____

Toners/astringents I'd like to try:

_____

_____

_____

_____

Moisturizers I'd like to try:

_____

_____

_____

_____

Anti-aging or age-reversing serums/wrinkle treatments I'd like to try:

_____

_____

_____

_____

Eye creams/gels I'd like to try:

_____

_____

_____

_____

Acne medications/preparations I'd like to try:

_____

_____

_____

_____

Exfoliants/scrubs I'd like to try:

_____

_____

_____

_____

Other products I'd like to try:

_____

_____

_____

_____

Questions I'd like to ask a beauty advisor/cosmetologist:

_____

_____

_____

_____

Your Skin Care Log

Perhaps you've used a skin care system before but just weren't diligent about it. Well, maybe you need a little help. That's why I'm providing a Skin Care Log, where you can record a week's worth of your skin care practices. At the end of the week, there's a place for you to also record any changes or improvements that you see, as well as any problems you experienced.

Skin Care log

Monday

Cleansing method (morning): _____
_____

Cleansing method (evening): _____
_____

I used this toner/astringent: (leave blank if no toner used) _____
_____

This is how I moisturized (day cream, night cream, etc.): _____
_____

Product(s) used

Eye treatments: _____
_____

Acne treatment: _____
_____

My skin looks: _____
_____

My skin feels: _____
_____

Problems I'm experiencing: _____
_____

Improvements I can see: _____
_____

*This form is reproducible.

Tuesday

Cleansing method (morning): _____

_____

Cleansing method (evening): _____

_____

I used this toner/astringent: (leave blank if no toner used) _____

_____

This is how I moisturized (day cream, night cream, etc.): _____

_____

Product(s) used

Eye treatments: _____

_____

Acne treatment: _____

_____

My skin looks: _____

_____

My skin feels: _____

_____

Problems I'm experiencing: _____

_____

Improvements I can see: _____

_____

*This form is reproducible.

Wednesday

Cleansing method (morning): _____

_____

Cleansing method (evening): _____

_____

I used this toner/astringent: (leave blank if no toner used) _____

_____

This is how I moisturized (day cream, night cream, etc.): _____

_____

Product(s) used

Eye treatments: _____

_____

Acne treatment: _____

_____

My skin looks: _____

_____

My skin feels: _____

_____

Problems I'm experiencing: _____

_____

Improvements I can see: _____

_____

*This form is reproducible.

Thursday

Cleansing method (morning): _____

_____

Cleansing method (evening): _____

_____

I used this toner/astringent: (leave blank if no toner used) _____

_____

This is how I moisturized (day cream, night cream, etc.): _____

_____

Product(s) used

Eye treatments: _____

_____

Acne treatment: _____

_____

My skin looks: _____

_____

My skin feels: _____

_____

Problems I'm experiencing: _____

_____

Improvements I can see: _____

_____

*This form is reproducible.

Friday

Cleansing method (morning): _____

_____

Cleansing method (evening): _____

_____

I used this toner/astringent: (leave blank if no toner used) _____

_____

This is how I moisturized (day cream, night cream, etc.): _____

_____

Product(s) used

Eye treatments: _____

_____

Acne treatment: _____

_____

My skin looks: _____

_____

My skin feels: _____

_____

Problems I'm experiencing: _____

_____

Improvements I can see: _____

_____

Saturday

Cleansing method (morning): _____
_____

Cleansing method (evening): _____
_____

I used this toner/astringent: (leave blank if no toner used) _____
_____

This is how I moisturized (day cream, night cream, etc.): _____
_____

Product(s) used

Eye treatments: _____
_____

Acne treatment: _____
_____

My skin looks: _____
_____

My skin feels: _____
_____

Problems I'm experiencing: _____
_____

Improvements I can see: _____
_____

Sunday

Cleansing method (morning): _____

_____

Cleansing method (evening): _____

_____

I used this toner/astringent: (leave blank if no toner used) _____

_____

This is how I moisturized (day cream, night cream, etc.): _____

_____

Product(s) used

Eye treatments: _____

_____

Acne treatment: _____

_____

My skin looks: _____

_____

My skin feels: _____

_____

Problems I'm experiencing: _____

_____

Improvements I can see: _____

_____

*This form is reproducible.

5

What's Hormones Got to Do with It?

While the topic of hormones and the effects of changing hormones in the female body are very complex, this chapter will be very simple. With the help of respected experts, I have tried to take some of the guesswork out of the overwhelming subject of hormones.

READING ASSIGNMENT

Read chapter 5 from *What's Age Got to Do with It?*

Based on your reading, do you think you may have a hormone imbalance? On the following pages you will find a series of self-tests to help you and your doctor determine whether you are suffering from an imbalance in your hormones. Once you've completed the tests, I encourage you to photocopy them and take them with you to your doctor's visits if your responses on the self-tests raise any red flags.

LOW THYROID (HYPOTHYROID DISEASE)

Please check each of the following that applies to you.

☐ I have recently gained weight, but I have no idea why.

☐ I am tired all the time, but I get enough sleep, so I can't explain why I'm so exhausted.

☐ My sex drive is at an all-time low. I just don't know what's wrong with me.

☐ My nails have become very brittle. They break so easily these days.

☐ I have horrible bags under my eyes. I've never had those before.

☐ My cholesterol is really high, yet there's no reason for it. My diet is healthy.

☐ I failed my Basal Body Test (a number lower than 98 degrees; see page 126 of chapter 5 in *What's Age Got to Do with It?*).

☐ I used to be chipper in the morning. Now I can barely get out of bed.

☐ My hands are always cold.

☐ My hair has unexplainably gotten thin.

☐ I sweat a lot, for no good reason. I don't know where that's coming from.

☐ I've always had such regular periods. Now they're so irregular, I can't predict when they'll start.

☐ Why is my face so puffy?

☐ I always had perfect skin. What is all this patchiness about?

☐ My skin has dried out—but I haven't changed my skin care routine at all. Why's it so dry?

☐ I'm so depressed, and I can't explain it.

☐ I can't take the cold! I've never been like this before.

☐ Where did my eyebrows go? They've become so thin, I practically have to paint them on.

If you checked five or more of these boxes, take this page to your doctor and ask him or her if hypothyroidism could be the culprit.

LOW OR IMBALANCED ESTROGEN

Please check each of the following that applies to you.

☐ I used to sleep like a baby. Now I just can't get to sleep.

☐ I feel so listless these days.

☐ I'd forget my head if it weren't attached to me!

☐ I feel anxious sometimes, but I've never been that way.

☐ I have mood swings.

☐ Sometimes I swear I have hot flashes, but I'm not even forty years old.

☐ I am fatigued all day long.

☐ I used to be a real go-getter. Where has all my stamina gone?

☐ I wake up soaking wet at night, but it's way too early for menopause.

☐ Quite frankly, I don't care if I ever have sex.

☐ My skin looks so dull.

☐ I've been retaining water recently.

☐ My breasts seem to have lost their perkiness.

☐ I've been experiencing unexplained back pain. I haven't lifted anything heavy. What's wrong?

☐ I have terrible pelvic cramps, and it's not even my period.

☐ I've suddenly started bleeding when I have intercourse.

☐ I've developed recent vaginal itching.

☐ I feel like my skin is crawling.

☐ I've never had yeast infections before. Now I get them all the time.

☐ Sometimes when I sneeze, I wet myself. What's up with that?

☐ Sometimes I "squirt" when I laugh too.

☐ For no reason that I can explain, I've been experiencing extreme vaginal tightness—and it makes sex very uncomfortable.

☐ My breasts are very tender.

☐ I have temperature swings—and mood swings.

☐ I don't feel very sensual anymore.

☐ I didn't know what a migraine was until recently—now I sure do!

☐ Why do I feel so uptight?

☐ I feel nauseated from time to time, for reasons unexplainable.

If you checked five or more of these boxes, take this page to your doctor and ask him or her if low or imbalanced estrogen could be to blame.

LOW PROGESTERONE

Please check each of the following that applies to you.

☐ I don't know what's going on with my periods. I have one, then miss one, have one, then miss two . . . I bet I only have three or four a year.

☐ No, that's not me. I'm just the opposite. Sometimes I have two periods a month. Why can't I be normal?

☐ My periods are really, really heavy. I'm always afraid I'll have an "accident."

☐ My breasts are painful.

☐ My breasts have lumps.

☐ I have the worst possible PMS.

☐ I spot for a couple of days before every period.

☐ I have cystic breasts.

☐ I have unexplainable anxiety.

☐ I'm not a nervous person—but I'm so nervous and irritable all of a sudden.

☐ I've been retaining a lot of water lately.

☐ I've gained weight for no reason.

☐ I am constantly fatigued.

If you checked three or more of these boxes, take this page to your doctor and ask him or her if low progesterone could be at fault.

LOW TESTOSTERONE

Please check each of the following that applies to you.

☐ My muscles have become flabby of late.

☐ My muscles have become weak recently.

☐ I don't have any energy anymore.

☐ Why do I feel so insecure?

☐ I can't make up my mind about anything these days.

☐ I can take sex or leave it (leave it, mostly).

☐ I hate my body.

☐ My pubic hair has all but disappeared—and I hardly ever have to shave my underarms anymore.

If you checked three or more of these boxes, take this page to your doctor and ask him or her if low testosterone could be to blame.

LOW DHEA

Please check each of the following that applies to you.

☐ I feel so stressed all the time.

☐ I don't seem to have the stamina I used to.

☐ Turn that music down! (For some reason, I seem to suddenly have a problem with loud noises.)

☐ I am constantly fatigued. It never gets any better.

☐ I'm never in a good mood anymore.

☐ I suddenly catch colds so easily. What's happened to my immune system?

☐ I can't remember what I had for breakfast . . .

☐ I've lost my pubic hair.

☐ My abs have become flabby.

☐ My eyes are so dry all the time.

☐ My skin has become very dry.

☐ I've lost interest in sex.

If you checked three or more of these boxes, take this page to your doctor and ask him or her if low DHEA could be at fault.

POLYCYSTIC OVARIAN SYNDROME

Please check each of the following that applies to you.

☐ I've lost a lot of hair on my scalp recently.

☐ I've suddenly developed a "mustache" (or other facial hair). I may have to invest in a bottle of Nair!

☐ I've noticed that I have to shave my legs more frequently these days.

☐ I've never had hairy arms before, but all of the sudden, I have arm hair!

☐ I've gained weight for no reason.

☐ I look really muscular all of a sudden—and I haven't done a thing to get that way.

☐ Where did all this acne come from? I'm not a teenager anymore!

☐ I've had a couple of miscarriages.

☐ I can't seem to get pregnant, no matter how hard I try.

☐ I got pregnant easily the first time, but now I can't get pregnant again.

☐ My skin is red, and I don't know what's causing it.

☐ I've developed insulin resistance.

If you checked three or more of these boxes, take this page to your doctor and ask him or her if polycystic ovarian syndrome could be the problem.

Changing Seasons

Now, ladies, we're going to switch gears and focus the rest of this chapter on menopause and the time leading up to it, perimenopause. Before you skip to the next chapter, let me remind you that perimenopause can begin in a woman's thirties. Most women begin perimenopause in their forties and reach menopause in their fifties, but altogether, what we are discussing here is a three-decade span. That covers a lot of you. And for those of you who are in your teens or twenties and have not yet begun to experience perimenopause, you still need to be aware and prepared.

Q: What is perimenopause, and what's the difference between it and menopause?

A: Menopause, according to the *Merriam-Webster's Collegiate Dictionary, 10th ed.*, is "the natural cessation of menstruation."[1] You know that you have reached menopause when it has been one full year since your last period. Perimenopause is the period of time leading up to menopause. During this time you will be noticing changes in your body, the things we discussed in your reading assignment for this chapter: mood swings, vaginal dryness, changes in menstrual flow, etc. This is the season of time that women are talking about when they say, "I'm going through the change."

Q: I may be going through menopause. How can I be sure?

A: Again, if you're going through something, it may be perimenopause, not menopause itself (technically, menopause is a one-day event: the day your period stops for good and you never have another). How can you be sure? Visit your doctor. But before you do, take the "Am I Going Through the Change?" self-test on the next page.

Am I Going Through the Change?

Place a check in the box next to each statement that is true of you.

- ☐ I am thirty years old or above.
- ☐ I am in my forties.
- ☐ I think I'm having "hot flashes."
- ☐ I wake up soaking in sweat in the middle of the night.
- ☐ I'm hot as a biscuit, even in the dead of winter.
- ☐ I have a hard time getting to sleep.
- ☐ I wake up often during the night.
- ☐ My skin has never been dry, but now it is.
- ☐ I never seem to be interested in sex anymore.
- ☐ Sex is not comfortable for me these days.
- ☐ I have a problem with vaginal dryness.
- ☐ I'm suddenly very moody. No one ever knows what to expect from me.
- ☐ I cry at the drop of the hat for no reason.
- ☐ I've been having heart palpitations recently.
- ☐ My husband says I'm awfully touchy lately.
- ☐ I've always been a happy person, but now I'm depressed a good deal of the time.
- ☐ I can't seem to control my bladder. (Sometimes I leak!)
- ☐ I've been having anxiety attacks.
- ☐ My periods have become extremely heavy. I bleed more than I ever have.
- ☐ I'm hardly having periods at all anymore.
- ☐ My periods have been abnormally light for a long time.

☐ My periods are really short these days—one or two days and it's over.

☐ I seem to be absent-minded of late.

☐ I never got headaches before, but I seem to have them a lot now.

☐ Sometimes I skip a period.

☐ My kids wonder what's wrong with me. They say I've turned into a grouch.

☐ I've never had belly fat, but all of the sudden I have a "jiggly roll."

☐ I'm suddenly getting urinary tract infections.

☐ I've become really forgetful recently.

☐ I can't seem to concentrate.

☐ My breasts are really sore, for no good reason.

☐ My face is a mess! I have worse acne now than I ever had as a teenager.

☐ Where's all this facial hair coming from?

☐ I've put on a lot of weight, really fast—but I haven't changed my eating habits.

☐ I could make a wig out of the hair in my brush! It seems like I lose more every day.

☐ My nails are so brittle, but they never were before.

☐ I've been bloated recently, and I can't explain it.

☐ I am so exhausted—and I stay that way, it seems.

If you checked seven statements or more, you may want to see your doctor. If you don't have a doctor, do your homework before going to just any office.

Good Question!

If your doctor confirms that, yes, you are experiencing perimenopause, you may suddenly be overwhelmed with anxiety. I always find it comforting to ask plenty of questions. Knowledge is the first step to your healthiest, happiest life . . . even with "the change."

Following is a list of things to discuss with your doctor so you will leave his or her office feeling better equipped to face the challenges that are sometimes associated with this very normal season in every woman's life.

Ask your doctor about:
- ☐ The benefits of acupuncture for perimenopause/ menopause
- ☐ Natural bio-identical hormones (versus synthetic hormones), in particular: estradiol, estriol, estrone, progesterone, DHEA, pregnenolone, and testosterone
- ☐ Homeopathic remedies (e.g., sepia)
- ☐ Physical therapies to help with perimenopausal discomfort
- ☐ Dietary recommendations
- ☐ Recommended supplements (other than those listed below, which you could ask about specifically)
- ☐ Lachesis mutis, glonoinum, and belladonna for hot flashes/perspiration.
- ☐ Magnesium and calcium for mood swings
- ☐ Evening primrose oil for mood swings, irritability, breast tenderness, and bloating/water retention
- ☐ L-theanine
- ☐ Things to avoid

You should also network with other women who have gone through what you're going through now. Do you have any friends who have reached menopause? Write their names here and commit to giving each of them a call to hear how they handled their symptoms, what worked, what didn't, and what doctors or therapies they recommend.

_____

(friend's name)

_____

(friend's name)

_____

(friend's name)

The library and the Internet both offer abundant, valuable resources to help make "the change of life" as seamless as possible. Investigate the various books and websites on menopause, but remember: always run everything by your doctor first.

ROBIN'S SHOPPING LIST FOR PERIMENOPAUSAL SYMPTOMS

☐ Fish oil

☐ Evening primrose oil

☐ Magnesium supplement

☐ Calcium supplement

☐ L-theanine supplement

☐ Sepia*

☐ Lachesis mutis*

☐ Glonoinum*

☐ Belladonna*

*Use these only under the care of a homeopathic expert. See _What's Age Got to Do with It?_, **page 127.**

Finally, have a talk with your family. Sit them down and explain that you have begun a very natural, normal process, one that will affect how you feel, and perhaps how you act and react. Explain the symptoms you may have. Assure them that it will pass. Most important, get them in your corner. The process of menopause will be so much easier if you have sought your family's support from the get-go.

I hope that, between the book and this workbook, I have answered some of your questions with regard to hormones, their effects on you, and ways you can manage your hormones, rather than them managing you. Now we're going to talk about what should be every woman's "crowning glory": her beautiful head of hair.

6

What's Hair
Got to Do with It?

You're eating healthfully, you've been working out, your skin is glowing, and your hormones are in check—and now you want a beautiful head of hair too, right? We women don't ask for much, do we? Fortunately, beautiful hair can be had with the right care, cut, and color (some natural, some not).

This chapter is going to be a fun, try-me-on chapter made especially for those of you who are ready for a change.

But first, you should read about some of my crazy experiences at the salon. It'll help you remember that it takes a balance between willingness for adventure and knowing when to say, "Stop!"

READING ASSIGNMENT

Chapter 6 from *What's Age Got to Do with It?*

So you'd like to try a new hairstyle but have no idea where to start? Let me help you.

First, start with people you know. Whose hairstyles do you simply adore? Take a picture of these folks and place those photos in the spaces on the "Cutest Hairstyles I've Ever Seen" worksheet on page 80 of this guide.

Next, go through various hair or fashion magazines. Did you find anything? Who's wearing a style that you think might work for you? Cut out photos and glue them in the spaces provided on the "Cutest Hairstyles I've Ever Seen" worksheet. Finally, take the completed sheet to your salon and talk with a professional stylist. If you don't have a stylist yet, don't worry. We'll work on that next.

Let's suppose that you don't have a stylist. Think of people you know personally whose hair you love. Go talk to each of them, getting salon/stylist names and numbers from each.

I love _____'s hair.

She goes to _____ at _____.
                     (name of salon)   (salon address)

Her stylist's name is _____

and his/her phone number is _____.

I love _____'s hair.

She goes to _____ at _____.
(name of salon)   (salon address)

Her stylist's name is _____

and his/her phone number is _____.

I love _____'s hair.

She goes to _____ at _____.
(name of salon)   (salon address)

Her stylist's name is _____

and his/her phone number is _____.

Now we're going to go through the phone book and the Internet. Look in the yellow pages at the advertisements for various salons, or search online for salons listed near your area. Do any of them stand out? Write the names of these salons here. (Writing them here will keep you from having to look for them again later.)

I'd like to find out more about _____.

Their address is _____.

The salon phone number is _____.

Their website is _____.

I'd like to find out more about _____.

Their address is _____.

The salon phone number is _____.

Their website is _____.

I'd like to find out more about _____.

Their address is _____.

The salon phone number is _____.

Their website is _____.

The Cutest Hairstyles I've Ever Seen

Place snapshots or cutouts below of friends, acquaintances, celebrities, or others whose hairstyles you may want to try:

Now go through fashion and hair magazines. Cut out pictures of any styles that you find appealing. Glue those photos here:

Take these hairstyle pages to your local salon and discuss the styles here with a professional cosmetologist. Get his or her opinion on how each style will work with your facial structure, lifestyle, and so on. Is the style high-maintenance, low-maintenance, or no-maintenance?

You can also try visiting TheHairStyler.com. This site also allows you to take your facial shape (oval, oblong, square, etc.), hair texture, and hair density into consideration as you try on styles. There are hundreds of styles and colors to choose from, and once you've made some selections, you can learn how to create and maintain the styles you like best. You can save your new look(s) to show others and to take to your stylist.

There are probably scores of websites like this one, but this is a good resource that I've found. Once you've gone to a website or two and printed your favorite styles, print and paste the photos here.

Maybe you really like your hairstyle and don't care to change it—but you sure could use a change of color. (Or maybe you want to do both!) What color should you use? As you read in chapter 6, before you color your hair for the first time, you should start by asking yourself a few questions.

What Do I Want in a Color?

Check the box next to the statement that best describes your expectations.

1. What do you want from your hair color?
   - ☐ I don't want to change shades; I just want to cover my gray.
   - ☐ I'm getting a little older, and for me, my dark hair is too stark. I'd like to go a shade or two lighter.
   - ☐ My hair color looks a bit drab. I'd like to darken it a shade or two.
   - ☐ I like my natural hair color. I'd just like to "perk it up" a bit. Maybe some highlights, or some streaks . . .
   - ☐ I'm such a drama queen, and I do everything big. I want a bold change to go with my what's-that-girl-done-this-time? personality.

2. How often do you want to have to recolor, or in other words, how long do you want your color to last?
   - ☐ My life is so busy! I don't want to have to recolor but once a month, just to cover my roots.
   - ☐ I want it to last a good while, but I still don't want it to be permanent. I want it to wash out eventually—just not too soon—so I can try something new if I want to, without having a head full of permanent color already there.
   - ☐ I'm a little more hesitant than all that. I want something that will be gone within just a few shampoos so if I don't like it, I can change it more easily.

3. Do you want to be salon dependent, or "you dependent"?

☐ I'm a do-it-yourselfer. Why would I pay a cosmetologist beaucoup bucks when I can do it myself for much less?

☐ Let the experts manage it. I'm too afraid to do it myself (or I don't have the time for that, or it's too big a pain to do myself).

4. How much are you willing to spend, per month, on your hair style and color?

_____

(insert a figure above)

NO-NOS FOR LUSCIOUS LOCKS

- Smoking—put down those Virginia Slims, for good!

- Chlorine/salt water—wear a swim cap.

- Extreme heat—apply heat protective products before drying, and use flat or curling irons on dry hair only.

POWER FOODS FOR TREMENDOUS TRESSES

- Carrots

- Dairy products (remember to choose low-fat products for your cholesterol's sake)

- Dark green (especially leafy) vegetables (e.g., kale, spinach, leaf lettuce, broccoli)

- Eggs

- High-omega-3 fish (especially salmon)

- Legumes (lentils, pinto beans, kidney beans, garbanzos)

- Nuts (especially Brazil nuts)

- Oysters

- Poultry

- Whole grains

Note: If you'll look carefully, you notice that many of these items have something in common. Can you guess? That's right! Protein. That's important, because your hair, ladies, is 98 percent protein.

What if you just want to experiment a little? What kinds of hair products/devices should you have on hand? On the next page I have proveded a little list to get you going. (You may not want to try all of these, but this list will at least provide a starting point of things to have handy.)

- Shampoo
- Conditioning rinse
- Leave-in conditioner
- Styling gel
- Styling mousse
- Combs / brushes / picks
- Vent brush
- Round brush
- Blow dryer (with diffuser)
- Curling iron
- Hot rollers
- Spiral curlers / benders
- Flat iron / crimping iron
- Hair spray
- Spray gloss
- Spray-on hair color or highlights (very temporary)
- Brush-on (or smooth-on) temporary highlights
- Clip-on hairpieces
- Hair clips / barrettes and other hair accessories

If They Could See Me Now . . .

You've finally got the hair you want! You've nourished it, pampered it, clipped it (maybe colored it), styled it . . . and now you want to doll up your face. That's what we'll do in chapter 7!

7

What's Makeup Got to Do with It?

Makeup is a gift to womankind, and as I said in chapter 7 of *What's Age Got to Do with It?*, "makeup" was probably one of the first words to come out of my mouth! I have a passion for the stuff.

Maybe you're already a seasoned makeup wearer, but you'd like to try something new. Or perhaps you wear makeup but are dissatisfied with your look and don't know what to do to get a look you like. Or maybe you've never worn makeup and don't have a clue where to start. This chapter will help you.

Now that you've completed the reading for this chapter, let's have some fun.

Q: I've never been good at makeup application. I'm not even sure where to start. What should I do?

A: Well, let me start by asking you a few questions. Who can you think of whose makeup always looks flawless? Whose lipstick do you like? Whose eye cosmetics would you like to try? Whose general look would you like to imitate?

Record your answers here:

I like the way _____ does her _____.
         (friend/acquaintance's name)   (eye makeup, lips, etc.)

I like the way _____ does her _____.
         (friend/acquaintance's name)   (eye makeup, lips, etc.)

I like the way _____ does her _____.
         (friend/acquaintance's name)   (eye makeup, lips, etc.)

I like the color of _____'s _____

                  (person's name)   (rouge, eyeliner, etc.)

I like the color of _____'s _____

                  (person's name)   (rouge, eyeliner, etc.)

I like the color of _____'s _____

                  (person's name)   (rouge, eyeliner, etc.)

Now, ladies, you're going to ask your friends about their products and record their answers here:

_____ uses _____ by _____

      (person's name)   (type of cosmetic)   (company/brand)

in _____ and she purchases it at _____.

    (shade name)   (store/salon/website)

_____ uses _____ by _____

      (person's name)   (type of cosmetic)   (company/brand)

in _____ and she purchases it at _____.

    (shade name)   (store/salon/website)

_____ uses _____ by _____

      (person's name)   (type of cosmetic)   (company/brand)

in _____ and she purchases it at _____.

    (shade name)   (store/salon/website)

Are there any particular problems you'd like to correct, using makeup or accessories? (Examples include: bushy eyebrows; red, blotchy skin; sallow skin tone, acne; I don't like my eyebrow shape; dark under-eye circles; etc.) If so, write these things here.

_____

_____

_____

_____

_____

Steps to Beauty

Let's suppose you have some product ideas but just don't know what to do with those products once you get them. Or let's suppose you don't have an idea at all. What next?

I again recommend, as I did in the companion book, that you visit a cosmetic counter or two. Many cosmetic/skin care shops or department-store cosmetic counters (e.g., Estée Lauder, Prescriptives, Clinique) offer free consultations. Stop by one of these counters and make an appointment (some counters offer on-the-spot makeovers). Their beauty experts will match products to your skin type (oily, dry, combination), tone (fair, light, medium, dark), lifestyle (casual versus high-stress), and desired look (natural, daring, or somewhere in between) and will apply these products to your face. Don't hesitate to ask a lot of questions, and make sure that each beauty adviser who works with you tells you exactly how to duplicate the look he or she created once you walk out of the store.

Another option is to pay to have a professional makeover. Visit a local salon that offers facials and makeovers. If you don't know where to go, look through the yellow pages or online, and write down the names of three salons whose advertising indicates that they provide cosmetic services. Record them here.

1. _____

(name of salon)

_____

(address)

_____

(phone number)

2. _____

(name of salon)

_____

(address)

_____

(phone number)

3. _____

(name of salon)

_____

(address)

_____

(phone number)

Make an appointment at one of these salons and see what great look your makeup artists can create. Be sure to tell the artist about any particular "corrective" issues you would like for him or her to address. For example:

- My eyebrows are uneven. How should I shape them?
- How can I hide these skin discolorations?
- My eyes are so deep-set. How can I bring them out?
- My eyelids are puffy. How can I minimize that?
- I have sad, doggie eyes. What can I do to fix them?
- How can I make my thin lips look fuller?

You get the idea. And in every case, I recommend not buying the mother lode of products right then and there. Wear the products for a whole day, glancing at the mirror to make sure you like the look every time you see it. (Or ask the makeup artist for samples you can try for a couple of days to make sure there are no issues with allergies, breakouts, and so forth.) It may be a bold new look that a has to grow on you. Or perhaps a well-trained pro has told you that you need a more natural look or that your appearance is dated. Do your best to listen, but if you don't like the look, don't buy the products. Only buy cosmetics that you intend to use.

Still another option is to visit websites that offer virtual makeovers, such as Taaz.com and DailyMakeover.com.

Finally, a variety of books offer makeup how-tos that can help you get the look you want, teaching you everything from how to maximize your eyes to how to hide blemishes, achieve a dramatic look, or shape the perfect eyebrows.

The Hunt Is On!

Now that you've got an idea of the products, colors, and accessories you'd like to buy, it's time to go shopping. On the next page is a handy shopping list you can tear out and take with you to the store or salon.

This shopping list has spaces for you to use to write in the names of brands and colors that you want to try.

Beauty Products Shopping List

Check each item below that you'd like to purchase, and record the brands/colors in the space provided.

foundation

☐ liquid

_____
_____

☐ powder-to-liquid

_____
_____

☐ loose (e.g., mineral) powder

_____
_____

☐ cream/gel

_____
_____

☐ concealer

_____
_____

blush

☐ powdered:

_____

_____

☐ loose

_____

_____

☐ pressed

_____

_____

_____

☐ cream

_____

_____

☐ gel

_____

_____

finishing powder

☐ pressed

_____

_____

☐ loose

_____

_____

highlighter/brightening product(s)

_____

_____

bronzer

_____

_____

color-correcting products (e.g., to tone down yellow skin tone, neutralize ruddiness, etc.)

_____

_____

lip primer (to keep lip products from bleeding or feathering and to give them extra wear)

_____

_____

lip liner

_____

_____

lip gloss (remember to choose products with sunscreen)

_____

_____

lipstick

_____

_____

eyeliner

☐ pencil

_____

_____

☐ liquid

_____

_____

eye shadow(s)

☐ cream

_____

_____

☐ powder

_____

_____

_____

_____

☐ mascara

_____

_____

eyebrow color

☐ pencil

_____

_____

☐ powder-to-liquid

_____

_____

Other Beauty Products I'd Like to Try

_____

_____

_____

_____

_____

_____

Accessories

☐ sponges

☐ lipstick brush

☐ blush brush

☐ powder puff

☐ powder brush

☐ eyebrow brush/comb

☐ eyelash curler

☐ tweezers

☐ synthetic eyelashes

Almost There . . .

Amazing! Your skin is beaming, and you're wearing just the right colors on your face—not too dark, not too light. Your hair is lovely, its shade a perfect complement to your skin and the cosmetics you've chosen. But you can't go walking about in the world "in naught but your skin"! You need clothes—the right clothes—for every occasion. That's what we'll look at in chapter 8.

8

What's Fashion Got to Do with It?

We want to look our best in our clothes, don't we? And the last thing we want is to end up on one of those embarrassing reality shows where someone tells us how awful we look in the things we wear and how dated our wardrobes are. Could you use a little help with clothing selection? Then before we embark on this workbook chapter, complete your reading from *What's Age Got to Do with It?* In the assigned chapter, you'll find a wealth of information on building a work wardrobe from scratch, accessorizing, dressing to look lean, and more.

Q: I've figured out my colors, and I have a pretty good idea of what styles don't look good on me. But I'm still not sure what kind of clothes would look best on me. I've been through all kinds of fashion magazines, but the information there just confuses me. Sometimes the writers even say conflicting things. I need some help deciding what to put in my wardrobe. Do you have any more suggestions?

A: Yes. Don't ignore the Internet. Search for websites that can help you make sound fashion decisions. One good site is My Virtual Model (mvm.com). There you can custom create a "model" who looks remarkably like you (same hair color, style, physical dimensions, etc.) and then virtually try on different outfits to find the right look for you. Another site that was easy to find was TryStuffOn.com. There are probably dozens more of these types of websites, and there are even sites for plus-size women. Take advantage of them.

A Few Fashion Tidbits

In addition to the material in chapter 8 of *What's Age Got to Do with It?*, here are a few fashion tidbits to help you make the right fashion choices:

"It is what it is."

Your body is your body, it has its good spots and its bad spots, and you have to choose clothing with its particular shape in mind. If you have broad hips, it does not matter how good your skinny sister looks in that flared skirt or those baggy trousers—you probably shouldn't do it. You may not want to wear clothing that bares a lot of cleavage, if you don't have a lot of cleavage to bare. If you feel that your legs are a bit chunky or perhaps too skinny, don't wear short skirts. You get the picture. Make the most of the body you have. It's your own; it's unique; and you can look beautiful in the skin you're in, by emphasizing the most flattering aspects of your figure. The right clothing selections should always make you look and feel beautiful.

Dress your age.

I'm a firm believer in doing and wearing what I want, and I choose to dress in ways that flatter me and my unique figure, regardless of what is "in" for my age group. I don't like to be told I'm "too old" for this or that. But, that said, there are *some* guidelines as to what is appropriate for your particular body at your particular age. The right clothes should look classy and sassy at the same time. So, if you're forty-five, your granddaughter's miniskirt may not be the best pick for you. Stay out of the juniors department! Likewise, if you're twenty-two, you don't want to dress like your great-aunt Aggie (who's seventy-eight and counting). Basically, it all boils down to using simple common sense when you shop.

Don't shop from the runway.

Ever watch one of those fashion shows, where stick-thin models sashay down the runway, looking as if they haven't had a home-cooked meal in ages? Ladies, please understand that what you see on the runway or in *Vogue* is not always meant for day-to-day wear.

Feelings . . . nothing more than feelings.

You can look drop-dead gorgeous in that fitted dress, but if it itches or is too tight to breathe, what good is it? You'll be miserable all day. Get clothes that fit your body now, not how it was five years ago or how you hope it will be. They can have a little breathing room, sure. But don't buy an entire wardrobe based on your plan to lose thirty pounds. Buying a wardrobe full of too-tight clothes is nonsensical (not to mention sadistic!). So get clothing, shoes, and undergarments that fit now. (See pages 199–200 in *What's Age Got to Do with It?* for tips on getting the right bra size.) You can always alter them later, if necessary, or build a wardrobe in your new size, a piece or two at a time, after you've lost (or gained) the weight you plan to.

Building Your Wardrobe

After all that you've read and heard, maybe you still need a bit more help. You know what looks good on you. Maybe you've even had a "profile" of some sort to determine what colors are best for you. But what do you need in your closet first?

On the next page, I have created a Build-Your-Wardrobe Checklist that you can use for your shopping excursions. This handy checklist contains the basic items most women need for work and leisure.

The Build-Your-Wardrobe Checklist

Startup Items

- ☐ basic black dress
- ☐ black pants (choose all-weather wool gabardine or similar fabric)
- ☐ black pumps
- ☐ black skirt
- ☐ white Oxford shirt
- ☐ white silky blouse
- ☐ jeans

Items to Add as You Go

- ☐ white slacks
- ☐ gray slacks

Here's a quick review (adapted from the "Answers from the Expert" section of chapter 8 in *What's Age Got to Do with It?*) on how to look your best, in spite of those pesky fashion "trouble spots."

- **Thick waist:** Wear tailored, well-fitted clothing—whether it's your sweaters, shirts, or coats. Choose ruched tops and blazers left unbuttoned, with a camisole or T-shirt underneath. Avoid empire waist tops, sturdy fabrics can disguise less-than-six-pack abs. Dress to show off your best assets (great legs; slender, attractive arms, etc).

- **Flabby upper arms:** Select bell sleeves, three-quarter-length sleeves, or button-down shirts with the sleeves rolled up just above the wrist. Avoid cap sleeves or sleeveless tops.

- **Pear-shaped lower body or large bottom:** Look for dark, boot-cut jeans with big pockets with stitching on them. Wear light-colored or fun, printed tops to bring attention to your upper body; a good, tailored blazer that hits at the hip; and higher-heeled shoes to make your legs look longer. Opt for A-line skirts and dresses to hide a full lower body.

- **Thick calves:** Dark hose or long leggings can help slim some calves, and for footwear, choose open- or closed-toe pumps in attractive colors. Avoid skintight leather boots and ankle boots.

- **Oversized bustline:** Begin with a minimizing bra. Then choose V-neck or scoop-neck tops or a blouse that's left a little open at the top. Avoid high necklines, closed-neck tops (like turtlenecks), and shirts with lots of ruffles, ruching, or puffed sleeves, as well as heavily embellished or breast-pocketed shirts. Emphasize a slim waist with a belt or sweater with a banded bottom.

- **Boy-shaped body:** Slim-fitting, tailored tops, and blazers that nip in at the waist can create the illusion of an hourglass figure. Define your waistline with ruched-waist dresses and tops, belts, and wrap dresses. Choose pleated or layered skirts. Avoid straight/pencil skirts.

- **Short frame:** Wear monochromatic clothing to elongate the look of your body. Choose high heels or platforms to add some lift to your body. Avoid huge necklaces and extra-large handbags and other accessories.

What's Faith Got to Do with It?

adies, we have almost reached the end of our journey together through *What's Age Got to Do with It?* and this makeover guide. This is the final chapter, and it's brief. But to me, it is one of the most important. In my life, faith has played a fundamental role in the way I approach my physical health. For me, it would be unhealthy to divide the two and assume that they don't have some impact on each other. In this chapter, I encourage you to engage with a faith element in your life and urge you to consider how crucial a healthy inner life is to a healthy body. As you consider these questions, I don't mean to pry or push you in any specific direction. But like a friend, I simply

want to throw the questions out there and give you the space to answer
them if you'd like.

READING ASSIGNMENT

Read chapter 9 from *What's Age Got to Do with It?*.

Some Questions to Consider

Instead of trying to analyze and log faith as we've done with our physical
health in previous chapters, I've found that sometimes the best thing to do
is just ask the question and answer it honestly. There's no right or wrong
answer here. This usually gives me a lot of clarity on things that are harder
to measure, things like the role of my spiritual life to my life as a whole.

• • •

What are you doing to create meaning and purpose in your life? What role
does faith play in your sense of well-being and your sense of purpose? Are
you drawing strength from your faith to live your healthiest, happiest life?

_____

_____

_____

_____

_____

_____

_____

If you're not a person of a particular faith, have you identified what gives you a sense of meaning and purpose? List some of those things below.

_____

_____

_____

_____

_____

_____

_____

_____

_____

_____

_____

_____

_____

_____

_____

_____

_____

_____

_____

_____

_____

_____

_____

Notes

Chapter 2: What's Fitness Got to Do with It?

1. Robin McGraw, *What's Age Got to Do with It?* (Nashville: Thomas Nelson, 2008), 17-18.
2. Ibid., 29.
3. Ibid., 37–38.

Chapter 3: What's Nutrition Got to Do with It?

1. For more information on the Food Pyramid, visit the official USDA website at mypyramid.gov.

2. Corinne T. Netzer, *The Complete Book of Food Counts*, 8th ed. (New York: Dell, 2008); Allan Borushek, 2008 *CalorieKing Calorie, Fat, and Carbohydrate Counter* (Hudsonville, MI: Family Health Publications, 2007).

3. Phil McGraw, *The Ultimate Weight Solution Food Guide* (New York: Pocket, 2003).

Chapter 5: What's Hormones Got to Do with It?

1. Merriam-Webster's Collegiate Dictionary, 10th ed. (New York: Merriam-Webster, 1998), s.v. "menopause."